Aging

Cheryl **Caldwell**

KPT PUBLISHING

When did "old" happen?

It seems to have
happened overnight.
Suddenly,...

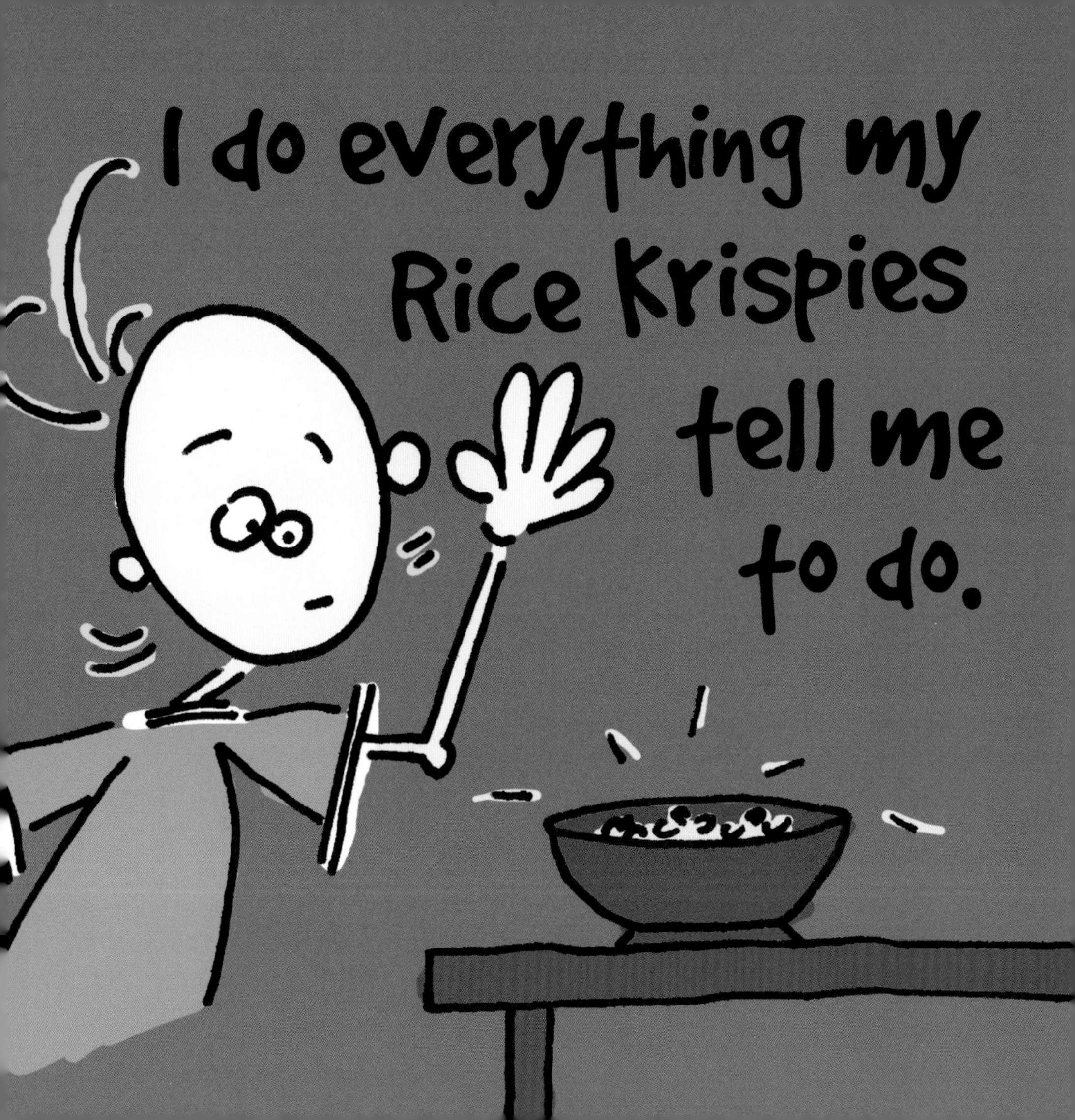
I do everything my Rice Krispies tell me to do.

You try to stay in shape.

I'm trying to lose **10** pounds.
I only have **13** more to go.

But you can't eat like
you used to.

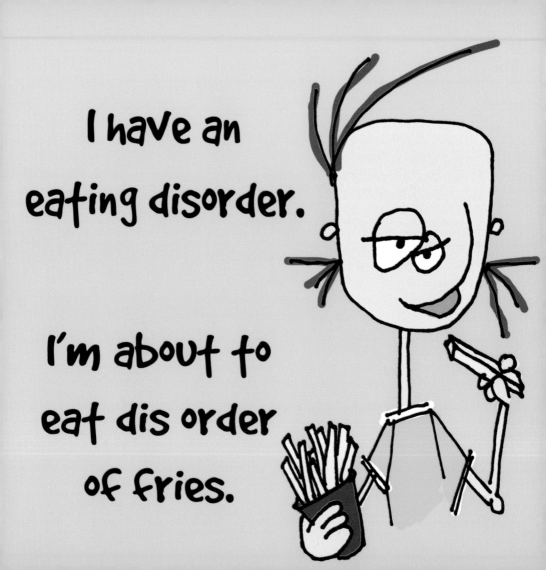

Working-out doesn't have the same result.

I ran for two minutes this morning but went back home because I forgot something.

I forgot I hate to run.

New clothes
don't help.

Neither does make-up.

Inside, you don't
feel any differently.

I'm old, but I
feel like I'm 20.
Then I hang out
with 20-year-olds,
and I'm like,
"Nevermind, I'm old."

But then, what is maturity, actually?

I'm beginning to believe
I will never be old enough
to know
better.

The outside is another story.

Your whole body is
telling on you.

You can tell a lot about a woman from her hands. For instance, if she has them around your neck, she's probably slightly upset.

The mind isn't behaving any better than the body.

Look on the bright side...

at least you're getting
your exercise.

Walk upstairs.
Why did I come
up here?
Walk downstairs.
Remember now.

Don't be one of those
old people who sits around,
talking about their ailments.

Take charge.

When I'm old, I'm totally going to be one of those old people who bites everybody.

Everything will be
blamed on your age anyway.

Had an argument in my head.

Made corresponding facial expressions.

Now everyone thinks I'm insane.

Have some fun with it.

The next time a stranger talks to me, I'm going to look shocked and whisper, "You can see me?"

Put a new twist on old things.

When someone begins a joke with, "Knock, Knock",

I respond, "It's open."

And create
built in reminders.

Find your inner-child.

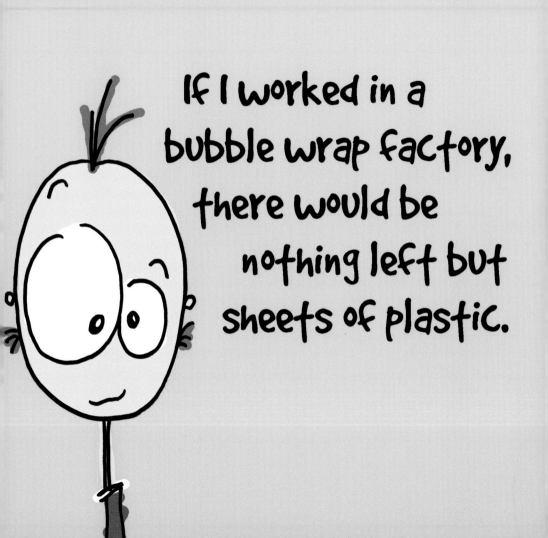

There's always
a positive way
to look at things.

Don't give in so easily,
because the truth is...

About the Author

Cheryl **Caldwell** is a sometimes artist, photographer, filmmaker, marine aquarist, and author. Most of her inspiration comes from her unconventional view of the world and the fact that she finds the mundane hilarious. She is owner of Co-edikit®, a humor based company that pairs comical illustrations with a witty combination of clear cut, down-to-earth words of wisdom and sarcastic humor. Her artwork and characters have been licensed and sold throughout the world. Her original paintings of the Co-edikit® characters can be found in several art galleries in the U.S., including Bee Galleries in New Orleans. She still subscribes to the philosophy that if you're having a bad day, ask a four- or five-year-old to skip. It's hysterical.

Aging

Copyright © 2017 Cheryl Caldwell

Published by KPT Publishing
Minneapolis, Minnesota 55406
www.KPTPublishing.com

ISBN: 978-1-944833-08-4

Design and production by Koechel Peterson and Associates, Minneapolis, Minnesota

First printing March 2017

10 9 8 7 6 5 4 3 2 1

Printed in the United States of America